The Thirteenth Iron Law

By

Mark R. Loiselle

First published by AuthorHouse 04/29/04

ISBN: 1-4184-5820-1 (e-book)
ISBN: 1-4184-3852-9 (Paperback)
ISBN: 1-4184-3851-0 (Dust Jacket)

This book is printed on acid free paper.

on response to the inner world and to the outside world or on the response of the inner world and of the outside world or on attitude.

About this Book

The Thirteenth Iron Law started to develop around 1990. The author started writing around then and says that to this day he does not understand why except that moving a pen on paper was fulfilling. Mark wrote The Thirteenth Iron Law in order of himself first, family second, the larger community third and beyond. It was not until the later stages that Mark could envision the book in such an order.

Mark views The Thirteenth Iron Law as a testimony to his particular community which is the community of those who deal with mental illness as he does. He says, "If life is about to swallow you grab it by the throat and never give up."

Respectfully So

He said to his friend,

"I am a product of my environment."

So they spoke, his friend first;

"You are made up of all of your experiences."

"But"

"No no, you are made up of all the choices you have taken as well."

"But I"

"No, you are made up of all the decisions in which you acted upon and what happened because of your actions in your lifetime up to now."

"I never thought"

"Yes! Do not lower your self by not taking ownership for what you are responsible for."

"Really"

"OK, and never trivialize your self my friend for your part in changing this world. You are responsible for helping to create a different environment."

"Thank You."

"Your welcome."

This Fine Young Tree

Spring had arrived at the nursery, and it was quickly becoming a busy place. People were looking and touching the trees. Choosing which tree to take home, or transplant, was a decision each would be making.

The cool night breeze carried a question from a young tree to its mother, its mother stood fifteen feet tall and was a short distance away. "Mother," the little tree called, "there were some men looking at me today, and one of them touched my leaves. What did they want?"

"Oh I was afraid of this," the mother of the little tree thought. She sadly spoke to the young tree saying, "You are a strong and fine young tree. You are the only tree within the nursery that has grown from a seed planted here."

The young tree questioned, "how can that be?"

The young tree's mother told a story. "One fall, a squirrel jumped up into my branches and took a seed from me and put it into its mouth. The squirrel then jumped back to the ground and buried the seed in the rich soil where you are now. The next spring, a tiny sprout came from the seed, and that was when you were born. You grew straight and strong and fast for such a young tree. The caretakers did not remove you as they would a weed, because you had those good characteristics. You may be going to a new home."

"But mother," said the worried young tree, "I don't want to leave you."

"It is alright," she spoke softly, "there is someone who wants to care for you."

Early in the morning, some men came to the nursery. They had shovels, an ax, burlap and twine. The little tree became fearful and called to its mother: "Mother, what are they going to do?"

"Don't be alarmed," she said, "they need those tools to move you properly so that you are not injured. You are going to a new home"

Suddenly the young tree yelled, "they are cutting my roots mother! I think I might die!"

"Don't be fearful," she said, "all will be fine in your new home, and you will grow new roots."

"Good bye mother," the young tree called as it was loaded onto a truck and taken away. "I feel like I am dying," thought the young tree, very much in shock from its uprooting.

The young tree was transplanted into soil different than that of the soil at the nursery. There were many nutrients added to the soil so the young tree would continue to grow fine, despite its being transplanted. The burlap was left wrapped tightly around its roots and the hole that it was put into was packed with rich fertilizer.

"I am on fire," the young tree thought. "My leaves are falling off. I feel like I am dying."

The young tree was indeed dying. A second shock - it's transplanting - had set in. The young tree stopped growing.

Two men were working nearby in the yard. Their nicknames were Coush and Cam. They saw the sick young tree and examined it. They discussed what they thought the problems might be. They talked about the young tree's root system. Coush decided to talk to an expert: an arborist. The arborist agreed with Coush and Cam. The young tree was dying because its roots were burning from a bad soil mixture. Coush and Cam decided to do their best to turn the suffering young tree back into the fine young tree it once was.

The young tree was so close to death that Coush and Cam had to act fast. They decided the most urgent matter was its root system. They knew they needed to cleanse its roots. They knew that washing away what was destroying it was imperative.

Each morning Cam, while watering the yard, would water the little tree for ten minutes. Soon the little tree lost all of its leaves. Some of its branches appeared dead. Coush came by one day and scratched the thin layer of bark to see if there was indeed any sign of life under it. He saw green and thought, "there is still hope for this young tree." Cam continued to wash the young tree's roots every other day.

Early one morning Coush and Cam were working in the yard. Cam was watering the young tree, and he was wearing a big smile. He called Coush over to take a close look at the tree. They looked at each other and burst into laughter. The young tree had sprouted hundreds of tiny new shoots on its main stem and on some branches as well. It was joy for Coush and Cam to see all their time and caring result in the rebirth of the young tree.

The young tree was left on its own for the rest of the season. It was a good growing season. During the winter Coush and Cam would look out windows and wonder if the young tree would survive the cold and snow.

Winter passed and spring arrived. The young tree appeared to have survived. Through the growing season Cam watered the young tree occasionally. Coush would look it over and think about its fall pruning.

As fall arrived Coush removed all the dead branches from the young tree, and there were many. He carefully selected the healthiest ones to remain. Those remaining were pruned to help the young tree grow outward and up. Coush worked with a painstaking effort; if he removed too much the young tree would die for sure. Coush finished his pruning with a touch up here and there in order to give the little tree some shape.

Springtime was a new beginning for the young tree. A show of bright pink blossoms were a compliment to a healthy cherry tree. This fine young tree came awake and thought, I smell wonderful and it is just like Mother said it would be.

That fall, Coush and Cam stood at a distance admiring the shape of the fine tree when a squirrel came hopping down a far path. It ran across the lawn and jumped up into the young tree. The squirrel played in the branches, then it came back to the ground with a seed in its mouth. The squirrel planted the seed not far from the young tree. The fine young tree thought, "everything in my new home is beautiful and it feels as though mother is still standing nearby."

A Fare Unfair

As he compensated for her diamond less finger with ordinary shoes his disregard was an empathy of the longing for oblivion never to be found in the silence of an anger endlessly expounded as those apathetic stood by hopelessly and knew but could not say so scribed.

And going back was a fear to loose his will of a good work while a voice cried in the wilderness of this message unaware of the yielding of a venom of a lifetime and followed to see good will and the beauty of its true work.

Negamation

Sleep misperception was once again true, as he rose at dawn one thing to do. Run a mile on the cool morning road and a sprint to an end would make the day feel new. Some of this and some of that, a bowl of cereal would surely do, then to kick off to school and meet his love true. She was in his energy a definitive love; she was why he lived and why he would hate, and in this world his heart would break.

Three meals he would eat before the clock showed noon. He had happy thoughts of his love and him alone together soon. Three half mile runs and jumping was his sport; thoughts of her in his mind were so clear. At the end of the day he caught the news, then off to sleep, and up again to repeat.

He didn't know, he didn't know, why those close to him would rage on him so. Was it pride in the good he did for himself, or the gossip untrue - what others wanted to see her do? He didn't know, he didn't know, he told himself... *I don't know.*

I don't know at the end of each sentence, those words he would speak, bringing doubt to his voice and all his words became weak. One day he awoke and ran no more, nor did he have love's open door. In such a habit, friends were lost, even friends from long before.

In a new beginning, a man did say, "Stop right there what you say. You must give your most to be aware. Understand that new friends are indeed out there."

So aware he became of those words: *I don 't know.* So he un-learned that habit and let those words go. To say *OK* was a new rule. Saying *OK* brought him back to before that bad way.

The one he so loved had gone astray. He missed, for so long, holding her slender body every day. But in the end, even that was *OK.*

At The Lot On The Job

The trees were a reflection and in a sway they seemed so far away as a busy day was in the making. There were the impoverished along with their saviors so well dressed and posed. They passed by together almost hand in hand. He wondered how could this be. Their walls were old brick and stone. The healthy and the wealthy were there as well and did come and go as a traffic of their own. They were a reflection within the trees as well and could be faintly seen. They walked by brass and oak to do their deeds.

The tending of matters brought many smiles to see as he tended the unseen gate. The gulls would circle in an updraft and some would depart in all directions. Crows accosting a hawk created a screaming chatter. Swallows were in their frenzied flight catching insects too small too be seen. Pigeons were eating what treats they could find. Mallards seemed to have the right of way when one lazy crane came drifting by. One lazy crane the only thing there that was seemingly sane.

The Storm The Stars And Play In The Yard

The chaos of the storm
A brilliant starry night
A prancing fawn
These things I happen upon

From a worn out pouch came a plea
In need of tender and from curiosity
One sunny day I felt a spark
My days to change for work in near dark
Now on my own
In a circle of joy
The captain was gone
With another far away storm

I looked to the sky
Into far galaxy showing
It's healing so real
And so I was smiling
So long it had been that sight to occur
So many years a faded blur

Now crystal clear this sky brought glee
A starry night once again to see

On route so neat another early morn

Eyes now caught one more treat

I sat and gazed

Was so amazed

A doe with fawn

Ten paces away

Prancing about

For the break of day

A show of light

Brought an end to their stay

I felt sad then glad

As They went their way

Storms shall pass and a clearing to be

A star lit night is a show for free

The pleasure of the fawn

All simplicity

A leaf on the wind falls to wither in the end

Another borne

One more journey to begin

Master Of Reception

A cheerful hello and clasp of the palms
Smile to smile to talk for a while
Seems so new yet recalling clear
Greetings are a continuous happening here

Writes til her hand
She can no longer command
Sits straight, appears tall
Talks an answer to the endless call

The files a very large part of her plan
For some moments a stretch in relief so to stand

She turns to grasp my stack of versed lines
A parcel unique in a binding so neat

To view her is a thought certain to be
A master of reception must be her degree

The Accommodation

Leader of healing
Urgent matters call trust
Making sets an adjust
For all those who must

Actions quickly combine
To search and to find
Another's ill self
To share in his mind

A comforting time for you is sought
Maybe high on a cliff
Or within only thought
To healing once more
Senses once again true
Your power in healing
The senses growing and anew

To Whom It May Concern, 8/17/97

I am writing to you in regards to a letter you sent stating that I am not eligible for financial aid.

In 1973 I was accepted into the liberal arts program at your college. In 1973 I was hospitalized with mental illness. During the Summer of 1973, as well, I attempted a class at the college but failed because I was unable to function due to powerful sedating medications. Reading was impossible as I was mostly blind because of those medications. I had to withdraw and I was hospitalized again. In the summer of 1974 I took the class again and although my vision was still impaired it had improved enough that I could read with a magnifying glass. I received a c for the class grade. I was hospitalized three more times the last in 1975. In 1976 I took a non-credit course at the college and withdrew as transportation was a problem beyond my control.

I hope you understand and agree that why I did not continue my education at the college was because of extreme circumstances. All is past now and I remain in outpatient treatment for bi-polar disorder and have remained stable since 1978. I have not been hospitalized since 1975. As I continue to get better to whatever degree I can find I have been successful in my endeavors since 1978.

I hope you consider this with my application for admission back into a degree program.

Sincerely,

14

The Continuous Growing Process

Hearing threatening voices, knowing they are for you: the pit of paranoia is low, self esteem is very real. It is affective.

The challenge is acceptance. Accept that they come from you, that you know they do. Push them back to where they came from, which is inside your own mind. Find the healthy part of you, or from where you will work from within yourself: your thinking and your body. Think the voices away and think restraint, or have control over what you allow your body to do.

When your self esteem is so low that bad thoughts about yourself become so powerful that they turn into a voice so loud it seems you can hear it from outside of your body, conscious thought is your weapon against them. Conscious thought is a skill we can teach ourselves with some work.

When you hear that voice, that bad remark about yourself, think the opposite. If for example you hear, "you are bad," consciously think at, or to, that voice, "no, you are bad." Of course the words you hear can be almost anything derogatory about yourself, and using the exact same words back at them is the way to combat them. Conscious thought develops as you hear the thoughts you summon on your own power against the voices of paranoia. In this way, you will develop your own personal brand of self-therapy.

Once you have developed conscious thought, it becomes a gift. It is the top of your thinking, which is the top of your mind, which is the top of your soul. You may have believed down to your soul that you are a bad person. And so must you think to your mind, to your soul, that you are not. And so you continue to grow. Your thinking self, if allowed, will grow until you die.

To hear voices that say others are against you to any degree is no fun, it is work. When you accept that it is your very own self, the process of taking responsibility for mending your self esteem can begin. Conscious thought is a gift waiting to be opened.

Fresh Air

Wide awake I turned to you as the day you love was far into night. We traveled far and I found you a room. I left before dawn in a walk eastward and soon into the forest I did march and continue and continue.

A yellow moon rose in the east as I stopped at the pass for a warm meal and the sight. Never a sight seen this moon so big. People stopped by to gaze a few minutes then leave.

Soon I was wandering once again down the road as I wondered on the brown bear I could see not far over there. My eyes had seen a star in the northern sky and no closer could I come to heaven this place so serene. I walked the highest land through the night as the moon turned to white as a light it lit my way. Now shadows it made of trees and brush to create a reverse image to capture me I was free.

By the dawn it had been twenty miles and a record of sort I keep. My worst enemy - the kangaroo mouse, if not for his teeth my snack of nuts in the plastic pouch would not be deplete. There were streams here and there so water was plenty. I cooked soup for a warm snack and slept less than two hours in all but four tries. I had turned my ankle before reaching the pass and thirty miles later I limped into town, the day before Halloween. I called for you by phone and you were in relief at my voice so you came to fetch me from my fresh air up there. Fresh air up there is like none anywhere so I try and try for you to as much for it care.

Dancing

Above the clouds
No sound of crowds
Under deep blue skies
Dark brown eyes

Through little drops of rain in flight
A pit of embers and fire light
Makes for the warming of this night
And so a dancing what a sight

So much more we do beget
This wild wood is now our set
Down the brook trees turn and whirl
Swept about by a wind to a curl

Memories in my mind as a book
Go back go back feel raindrops fall
Dance again in memory of it all

Dilemma

Allegory viewed
Growing and in a soft breeze
A delicate appearance
Fancy tinsel only in my mind
No other of such kind
None other to find
Grassy like objects
Ten thousand beads of light
Gotta fight gotta fight

A forest in my mind
To my knees around and behind
So much in fear
No help to find

A new insanity
An inner feud
Can't subdue
Exacting a toll
Four days past
Again and again
I won't keep it in
I won't keep it in
Over again I shall never begin

Languor

Been so long
Hurting inside
Need to be held
Not be let go
A pat on the back
Can't do it myself
Not no more
Where is a door
Can't go on
Must be gone
Can't believe anymore
Even myself
I'm starting to melt
Can't be gone
Control is hard
Makes me mad
Seems for real
Gonna loose it
Just can't choose it
Where'd the light go
Can't see no more
It's been so long
Been hurting inside
Can't run and hide
Need a healing ride

Let Her Go

For weeks you sit and think of her
The words you write for her do say
A love through night and work through day
For you she lives her lonely way

Each word is thought
Each line a part sought

Worked and re-worked she is about
Thought and re-thought beyond any doubt
Brought to a whole
That part of your soul
Pushed from safety and unaware

Long as it took to let it go
It's death is your living
I grieve it all so

Belief In Action

For years, I watched the roller blades weaving in and out: weaving in and out on sidewalks in the city. It was graceful to watch, but I thought, "no too dangerous," and had that gut feeling. That gut feeling told me my thoughts were true.

I could not sleep well at night, and a friend told me the nighttime may be the right time to learn, maybe early in the morning before the traffic and the people. Maybe then it would be safe. I started to believe the idea. The season turned and the sales began, so I asked questions about equipment and prices to become knowledgeable. It was recreation that I wanted as I thought of ice skating, something I did well.

As I entered the shop I was unsure and fearful. It was an unknown place with so many choices. But I was happy and secure as I left with the roller blades that fit so well around my feet. While I was sitting on the curb and fastening the many buckles, my heart beat with excitement.

With my shoes tied over my belt, I stood up and decided I would skate at least a mile back to the town line and take a cab home.

Standing up, I fell back to learn that the blades would slide forward from under me. Being determined, the thoughts of caution told me to take my time, take it slow, and make my way out of the lot. Hopefully I could make it onto the access road behind the plaza and be in a safe place to practice. When I skated onto the road leading to the plaza, some valuable techniques were learned.

22

Looking like a straggling beginner, and probably looking foolish, were not a concern as I learned to balance on the backs of my feet in order to turn. My arms would fly out of control from time to time, as I realized that what I had seen so much of others and thought was graceful was in fact also practice.

On the main road to the town line I nearly fell several times, and I was fearful but still determined. If I stayed on the shoulder of the road, it was more likely that I would dangerously fall, but the moving traffic might keep me off the road. The ideal surface was indeed on the road. It was mid day.

A gas station marked the town line, and my goal was in sight. Under a bridge I first lost my sight in the shade, and in fatigue. Again fearful but determined, and now with a passion to reach my goal, I passed the town line and would not stop.

"A cold drink would feel good," I thought as I plugged on up a small walkway aside the road. At times, my arms were still occasionally flying up out of control from rolling off the walk onto a grass shoulder. I was driven faster with the desire to reach the top of the two hundred foot walk.

I was twenty feet from the intersection where I planned to cross to a café for refreshment, and began to slow down when my blades slipped out from in front of me. I was tossed up, and fell down hard. I thought I threw my shoulder out as I came down hard on my elbow. I almost made it to the intersection and the café.

I lay on my back spread eagled, as passerby's in cars called for me out of their windows. I nodded to each while catching my panting breath. "I'm OK," was all I replied.

I sat up after some time and removed my new roller blades to put on my sneakers. I walked across the intersection to the café, the café being a well known steak house, into the rest room. As I cleaned the blood off my arms and hands, I knew I would need padded protection the next time I went out. As I sat at the bar, three soft drinks and a crock of onion soup was my reward for making it through. Then I relaxed to a soft summer like breeze and indulged in a cigar, and I thought while waiting for a taxi cab to take me home. I thought in my peace, "if I am ever up this way again I will push my way up the grass aside the walk, and I will work my way to the intersection and the café once more." I thought, "I will probably fall, but I will try. And if I fall, I will get up once again."

Accordingly

To love ones self is not conceit
To know the word accordingly

Accordingly only healthy things to do
Loving ones self is to love another true

About yourself have you looked to see
Truth is all about you individually

Step outside and look back to say
Do I see Do I see … Do I really see me

Hills And Valleys

Two souls of venture marching in time
In such motion soon to find
Hills and valleys then a long wind
Their hopes of a friend soon to find

Upon a surprise they stop what a sight
Behind a kettle and looking up in delight
Visions and thoughts came to delight
Together to be with to
Share with tonight

Stirring and pouring talking in hurry
The days of times past full and
They were merry
Until stew and all
Brought them to sleep
Dawns awakening was slowly complete
More visions and thoughts of
Adventure sure as of
These two
Their love and lure

With hopes next pause will be so kind
Hills and valleys marching in time

Belief

Believe in yourself and
Family dear
Friends that are true
All close when you're blue

Believe in the night
To walk under the moon
Under the circle of love to
The morning dove

Believe in the children
Your love is theirs
Castles in sand
A joyous hand

Believe in your parents
Love inside wisdom
Their eyes much know
To slow walk they still grow

Mountain peaks
A goal to you
Think feel and do
What is true what is real

About My Lamp

As I watch all the insects about my camp light I think what a lure to them this cool night. They must see it above and away from afar so I sit here and wonder just what they all are.

I love it here in this home so keen where giant mosquitoes are easily seen. Friendly they are as they come to land, even this one sitting here on my hand.

Viewing for some time it is such a wild sight. Moths fly by feel the heat and go right. On my left hand is one that looks like a fan it has gold wavy marks on shiny wings the whole span. A ruby red something comes to sit by and between hot and cold I think he's a happy guy. Just hanging around no interest to fly, another taste of coffee I think I will try.

A tiny wasp has caught my eye and no food is around he just sits without sound so of all things here another friend is found.

Two days ago it rained awhile and yesterday was warm I wore a smile. Tonight the stars show above my camp and filled with interest I look about my lamp.

Chained

He had been so long in a sort of dream. He was fighting what just could not be seen that he could once again do what would really mean. Hurting so long lonely images in his mind blue were only to be. He thought about then, that when, what he so wanted to be now. In a dwell all alone one friend just known could hear his despair and from his home a light had shown. With honor with hope a horseman rode to find almost gone his hurt his dream not owed. Not the weight of his son was heavy but the grasp on hope was a prayer for the self hater. He talked about being loved and he smiled at his new friend and talked about new plans. He knew to live was to unlearn - but how? He knew where honor had been and was gracious.

He looked in mirror to see time gone by made a dream turn pale and his worth fading away. In his quiet time a renew meant he wanted tomorrow with no more sorrow. Now his hope about when begins with now not the sadness about then and what made him so pale still dwells within, chained, and wanting to begin.

Light A Candle

Lost and hopeless no feelings of me
Only the memory like a whirling roar
That I had heard the day before
That day before when fear was me
So then only to be I could not foresee

So few a day of inner peace would be
So long unmoved silent rage did stay

From only to be
To aware and see true
The bad and the good
To understand my weeping should
And from the grays came clear insight
A beacon to me that night
And you the source I take flight
I take flight

From The Altar At Francis Gate

Completely aroused

Filled with affection

Ecstatic with encouragement

Compassion for the oppressed

Ruler of the merciful

Maker of hope in the soul

Completely dutiful and free to expand

Taught not to hate but nurtured of love

To laugh is to be strong

Strong with joy

Flying free

Validating self-regard

Driven to live these as truth

Into only such reality

My world alight with you

Living on within me

When I Want To Write

When I want to write but
Have nothing to say
I sit and crave for a
Fulfilling day

When I see my pen and
Wonder when
When my hand will find
Ideas on the wind

When I sit at night and
Hold the yearning the
Passion strong to
Learn along

When the lack of event calls for
One more walk I
Write about nothing and
Even with this it seems
Time well spent
I'm glad I could have this
Talk as it went

Mirror Of Toil

he thought of parents

As a garden grows so very strong
A harvest born did come to reap
And so is seen all things are right
A growing day a quiet night

When home became a weary place
We began to sing all sang along
Then we went among each field
And none another came along

The way it was
And such a way
The garden grows
Sunshine and fine days

So much in gratitude
Are we for you
Your love is mirrored
Your gardens grow

Hello Cousin,

We never talked much and I think that's Ok. I heard you have
been stuck for a long time. I understand what that feels like. I've
been stuck as well.

You probably heard that I have a mood problem. I used to get an
elevated mood and then crash into a major depression. I was
hospitalized five times because of it. I was confused and full of fear
in the hospital. People asked me in a matter of fact way - how do you
feel about that? What seemed to be the problem with this question
was that I had so much anger on top of older anger I just had one
feeling, the feeling of depression. Each event that caused anger I had
to keep inside because I was never taught the good things to do about
anger. Frozen rage is another name for depression. So how was I to
answer how do I feel when all the feelings I had kept inside became
one?

Among the difficulties I had in the hospital was to overcome the
stigma. I thought I was not like them until my treatment really
started. I realized that they had the same feelings as me and they were
thinking people as well. Later I learned that all of humankind share
the same feelings. It took time to sort out the events that kept me
from dealing with my life - that made me angry.

There are around 15,000,000 people in this country right now who
are in treatment for depression. You are not alone. Depression is a
mental illness that still carries stigma, or, a mark of shame or
discredit. People who stigmatize others are judgmental and nobody

has the right to try to teach another that any of the myriad of feeling are not valid. So be careful of who you trust with information about any events that activated your anger and rage - your depression. The bottom of it all is we are sensitive and fragile beings. Depression is an illness of the mind and because we could not deal with experiences, for whatever reason, the stress in our minds finds it's way into our bodies. Depression is a physical illness as well.

When I was in the last year of high school I was married, my wife was expecting our child, I was working full time at night, I was living away from home for the first time in an apartment, I had a full blown specific and social phobia, I had not yet learned how to take care of myself. Wheeeew! I collapsed at work one night. I broke. There were too many lifetime changes at one time. Five lifetime changes at once and a devastating phobia on top of all the anger I had kept inside. If I could not take care of myself how could I possibly care for those I needed to care for. Take care of yourself first. As long as what you do is good or health towards yourself other people do not matter. You need to care for yourself during this time. Healthy self regard is necessary for you to live a meaningful good life that only you define. Put aside the rest of the world for now but keep in mind it is against the rules to hurt someone to include yourself in actions out of any feeling. When I started to focus on myself and stay away from those who distract me from getting better I started to get better.

If you have been offered medication understand that they may be a tool or they may be replacement parts you will always need. Be aware of what they do as most doctors can only put them in the ball park and a good doctor wants to know from you how they are affecting you.

There are good support groups out there and the people that go to them share our feelings as well. Finding neutral friends to support you is like shopping for a doctor. Any group where people complain about personal problems will only give you their problems, avoid these kinds of groups. If you feel like you have work to do when you leave it is a good group. If you feel better when you leave than when you arrived then it is a good group.

Above all be patient with yourself. It took us a long time to become ill so it takes time to work through all the things that we could not.

Take Care

My Dear Sister, 4/12/96

In reply to your interest about what has been happening with my treatment thank you for caring. I am expecting a letter from the rehabilitation commission in this state. I had a meeting and a woman asked me if I would rather have a physical or a sit down job. I told her physical but I don't think she understood that I have a sleep disorder that no doctor has hope for. Because of that I have a problem putting myself into a schedule. Even volunteer organizations demand a schedule. It is what I am left with after all these years. The lady did say that they could determine me unemployable but I believe that as long as I can think and move I have choice -there is hope.

You might find this current medication chart interesting:

Lithium

Depakote

Synthroid

Klonopin

Mellarill

Cogentin

Risperdal

Prozac

Benadryl

Clonidine

Zantac

Wow weee Huh?

The doctor is trying to remove the melarill and replace it with a safer drug but I get exhausted and then I get stomach spasms. The spasms are brutal as the pain radiates up through my chest neck jaw and ear. Cold liquid stops it but I have to be in a place where I can get it fast. Being a nurse you can probably understand what can happen if I injure myself such as a turned ankle or back strain. I can't take muscle relaxers or pain killers for more than two days on top of all those medications. It's a job to manage it all as my insurance says I have to be at the end of a refill before I get another. They do not run out at the same time so I make up to four trips to the pharmacy a month. It all allows me to keep active. It all helps keep me out of the hospital - twenty seven years now means something you know. There is a large population out there that believes getting better means losing all their support. Truth is getting better does not mean being cured.

Well it was good to hear from you. Keep on healing people and write again.

Dear Mom And Dad,

I was reading something interesting tonight and when I was done I wanted to leave my world. Don't be too alarmed you see there can be no schedule in my life. I can not be a part of the workforce because of this. This is not my fault. So you see my life is chaotic and I am not one to do nothing. I can not just be. Soon I will travel to the mountains where I will camp as long as I can. Probably not more than a few weeks though. Nature is most orderly and my home will be simple. Staying warm, dry and comfortable are most important and so fundamental up there. Schedule seems to evolve, wildlife awakens me before dawn. Coffee, food, a hike and a bath in the river with sand as soap - refreshing. Gathering wood, making fire and toasting food brings relief and seems always a pleasure. At night the darkness is a natural, sleep prompt and I may write by the lantern. A full moon is scheduled and will bring the desire for a late night walk - no lights necessary.

So I'm looking forward to leaving the chaos of nothing even if it is only for a few weeks. Just thought I would share this with you before I left. Think of me.

Take care.

She said, "I talk to my son about adult subjects" but he said, "that is empty knowledge he will not understand he is a child." He said, "you must talk to the child as an adult so as an adult do not say no or don't but rather speak in terms of the definition of the words don't or no and he will surely speak back to you as an adult and be a growing child. You see everybody deserves reason, everybody to include you."

Mary Lou

From here to there and again back around the fun is so frantic as you stood your ground So here you are in one bound upon the wall and so proud sitting next to me seeming almost as tall.

Off again to explore in dress of purple the great hall with bows and ribbons smiles and all more fun for you awaits I know excitement your moving is a call.

Back again and what is wrong your pretty ring lost as you played along look here and there yes I know it's not fair if you go far your mother must be aware.

Once again by me and sad I see let me say these words from me, you see it is not the matter of the ring so much but what it means in your tender heart is a treasure you see that will never part.

Open The Day

There is the night
When your tears fall alone
There is the darkness
That will not take your pain

What is the sadness in your day about
About the sadness you fade away
The darkness is deep don't go away
To sing slowly too
Sounds the color of blue

Where your body leans is a wearing mind
When you try to forget is sudden a weep
When love finds it's way to
Open just one day
Only leaves you alone and cry you to sleep

By The Ocean

A day so early and off to play
A day so early we strolled away

Waves crashed in a misty splash
Coming and going the ocean was rolling

Close together in a chilly mist
Holding each other was swiftly a kiss

Back we rambled as the tide was too near
Back we rambled the day was here

In Island

This lonely house in gloom
Casts the view of her aging away
Woman of years spent sits alone
Passing thoughts of her years gone by and
Possessing each hour
Her heart heavy does not show
But alone and in silence she weeps as
Her tears follow pathways of
The age on her face

A draft starts a clatter and
Calls her to slowly detach to
Edge slowly and in struggle and
In want to distract but
All sound once again fades to
Loneliness once again and
She prays for her aloneness
In its finality

Shattered Glass

learning hatred

racism

Anger came and once again hurt
A wound close to her soul
Holding it in and looking to go
Shattered glass in part was her story told

Never strike back so she was told but
Hatred at play took the joy of her day
The truth in sadness were
Her words so deep and
The slow sweet voice fell into a weep

As the tracks of her tears
The courage of self regard were
The words of her mother;
Your skin is so very well made
Most important your esteem
You must always save

Shattered glass to pick up
A child's ball let it lay
And the boy down way
Easy picking
On shaded skin is a mystery
Still today

A Different Path

He desired to give something to his friends since they were in need, but he had nothing to give. He became angry at his uselessness, but he could walk. So he left his friends to travel the road alone. For a while he moved along the roadside when he came to a fork. He chose the road to the right, and soon he found himself at the door of a little bakery. He was thirsty by then, so he ventured inside to ask the shop keeper for a glass of water. He sat in a corner with his filled cup and tried to think all that was wrong.

A short while had passed when he was asked by the shop keeper if he desired a biscuit, but he had no money. So he informed the man. The shopkeeper smiled on him saying he had made too many, and in the morning when they would no longer be fresh, he would not sell them.

He thought of his friends as he looked at the many golden biscuits left on the shelves. He needed to leave but stopped at the counter to look at his change. The man appeared, put some biscuits into a bag and gave them to him. He looked down to see a cup on the counter and let what little change he had fall into it. The shopkeeper took back the bag and filled it overflowing with the golden biscuits and handed it back to him. He was overjoyed upon leaving the shop and decided to return to his friends.

His friends were surprised and happy to see him. He emptied the bag of biscuits on a table. They all enjoyed the tasty treats, and he was happy to be with his friends again.

The shopkeeper cleaned the cup to shine and put it back on the counter. He smiled as he looked at the remaining biscuits on the shelf. The man then closed his shop and left for home.

As the last of the biscuits were eaten he thought that he had been on a dark road and found a light on a different path. He knew he had to enjoy the moments with his friends. He wondered what road he would take when he had to leave once more.

We Just Try to Help

the workshop

Feelings were ripping our hearts as

We cried

We kept the hurting alone and inside

We thought it would mean to slowly die

We only found a crutch that would lie

We could not be aware of why

Our souls then called for truth to find but

Our worth without, was first in mind

So then we felt our world unkind

Looking in mirror seeming a mistake

Hope then came for us to make

Soon we turned our hope into faith

Now feelings for us we soon could reap

A flowing stream from inside so deep

And a voice within we all did hear

Listen closely to another's fear and

Understand the other's tear

Wendy

The wind it cried of sadness and the wind it filled with sorrow. Soon we all were here to see that Wendy would come to be.

Wendy was like a butterfly from the breezes caught in a web. We watched her as she fluttered there and let simple words be shed. There she was in her lonely way as we sat close by and gazed. Soon we found we were all the same as we listened to whispers seemingly call her name.

Looking up we were all in smile and viewing a wondrous sight. Our catch our Wendy was freed again with the breezes now she was taking flight.

We knew being caught up in our ways just should not stay and breezes would whisper for us to say, guide all your Wendy's through their days and let sounds of crying be sadness away.

Hello There

This is a little hello to you

It is sent you see to so very few

Just for you now this is true

While listening I would be so blue

Your spoken word

Straight by me flew

Although your voice indeed was you

There seemed much more for words by you

So now my senses peak

Your knowledge now is

So much more sweet

Now I think you're so very neat

So hello I say to you this way

Maybe to each other we can find

Thoughts to share in our own time

And hear what we really have on mind

Make a present together

To be forever

By The Phone

Marshal's frustration was a compromise to the discussion and took some time to realize. "The problem is not with the ones that we know of but rather the ones that fall through the catch net." The discussion having only to do with what may be controllable. Funds above all could not be discussed.

It took some years for him to understand exactly what Marshall had been talking about, that the problem was about people not money. If someone or a system paid another to be the friend of someone close to despair was that person truly a friend. Would that person be there when that one reached despair and fell through the net to his or her end as to despair is to die. How to love that person in the way that person was not seemed the fitting topic for the discussion not how to impress more control by way of authority and power. So he wondered if that power would be based on distorted feelings, or rather, corrupt.

As he reached for the phone he felt the presence of hope and that was good but he stopped. He thought until he understood that what was had not changed and realized that every place he became trapped in was not of his own design. He felt as if he was being tested maybe by his conscience maybe by God. He thought these feelings were only that - feelings, valid but untrue. He knew he needed a plan and rose above the feelings of unimportance to indeed call for reassurance - the net to catch him and a plan only for his self. He told what was and its impact on him by the phone… his lifeline.

Iced Coffee, Peanut Butter And Jelly

Be he to become ill and lcose decision
Be he lost and decisions ill
Be you to find him loving what was not
Be you friend and ask you not

One mind lost
One mind will cost
One mind apart
One mind each a work of art

When is reason
When he hides his pain
There is an angel
Now he acts on today

Who is no reason but only excuse
What is excuse but not to decide
When is the answer for why he hurt and
Then is the gray day by day

Best Friend

Among our challenges we found each other
To find integrity fighting to see clearly
A clouded beginning born of fear
From a place where others were of the same
Together time gave friendship a name

Sharing the difficulties hours it took
As we worked to put one cover on a book
And on a shelf so neat it did look
Best friends you and me
I know you see
Each of our own opinions some set in stone
But trust in you and so you in me too
Few in a lifetime can truly be
Understanding you and too you of me

In a call late at night you know my plight
And at the door you were
So happy a sight

Tomorrow for fun a two hour hike
Twenty minutes to share
Through the phone friends alike

Dancing

Above the clouds
No sound of crowds
Under deep blue skies
Dark brown eyes

Through little drops of rain in flight
A pit of embers and fire light
Makes for the warming of this night
And so a dancing what a sight

So much more we do beget
This wild wood is now our set
Down the brook trees turn and whirl
Swept about by a wind to a curl

Memories in my mind as a book
Go back go back feel raindrops fall
Dance again in memory of it all

She Wants The Sky

Love letters make eyes sparkle as
Painted lips once again smile

She cares for herself
Thinks her way to health
Clean and made new
No longer blue

All that she owns
Rewards for hard work
These things do tell
Crystal, teak and gold all swell

In direction with a passion
Never to do another wrong
Strong indeed
Sad memories do not lead

Her energy high
No longer shy
Another's need
Never passes by
Wants the sky
She surely knows
Her house is why

The Lesson Of The Ash

Dwelling in the magnificent forest of giant ash trees were the Mendap, and they were a peaceful people. A great distance away west were the Celestereen: mountains of the stars that stretched as far as the eye could see. The summits that were never viewed as they vanished into the heavens, gave the mountains such a worthy name. From the edge of the forest, the fields and shallow valleys lay before the rolling foot hills of the vast elevations. The streams that rushed from the high steeps joined to form the river Osholan, which ran through the forest. This was the land the Mendap had called their home for hundreds of years.

There came a time when, in far fields, a settlement was observed. Over the years, a city of tents had grown. The people of the fields became known as the Raone. The valleys and streams provided plenty for all.

The people of the wood offered the Raone friendship, and their coming together was believed to be good by all. They organized a festival. There was much feasting and talk in the city of the Raone. The Mendap were excited upon returning home, as another celebration was fast approaching: the celebration of the harvest moon. Indeed the fields proved bountiful once again to produce the next flattering yield.

The Raone had learned that a treasure was hidden deep inside the home of the Mendap. Traveling among them, news was spread that the treasure would bring warmth during the colder times. About the land, such hard times would last through the time of the shaded daytime light, or from harvest to the sowing of fresh seed.

On the second day following the feast, a plotting of dark deeds began to obsess the Raone. Taking the treasure of the Mendap formed in their minds, and an evil pressure moved the desire deep. They decided that they would move in the morning before any light would show.

The Raone tried to sneak their way into the home of the Mendap, but it developed into a massacre. Death came to all except one called Rey, the son of Onwey.

Onwey was the strength and wisdom of and within the people of the wood. Rey rode in horror on Drapo, his fathers steed. Following the shoreline of Osholan, Rey wandered for a long time. He was alone, and he was lonely. Rey questioned his destiny.

At the edge of the river, the Raone came to a halt. Across a sheer cliff cut smooth by the river for tens of thousands of years, was the Wall of Alling. The treasure they sought in a frenzy of destruction had been found. At the same moment, a flawless crystal that stood perfectly straight above the tallest of the ash was found by the Mendap. It could not be moved.

It was mid-day when the source of all life fixed in the heavens, and the Mendap called Sey sent out a ray. The white light that reached the crystal was so majestic. From the crystal burst a beam of yellow light, which splashed upon the Wall of Alling.

The Raone watched in awe and became dazed in wonder. Their anger turned to sadness. They were shamed that the treasure would not be plundered.

A number of men, whose eyes were fixed on the wall, read out loud the words of Sey that slowly appeared: Reflected in your children is the toil of the good, and in their time the world will once again be as it should.

The Raone looked about and thought, "what have we done." Onwey lay slain beneath the crystal of warmth with no weapon in his hand. The crystal could not be taken as it belonged to Trail, father of Sey, and the maker of all that would come to be. The crystal could not be taken.

The Raone left the forest. From time to time Atpo, the strong and most wise of the Raone, would return to the forest to reflect. He deeply felt the shadow of guilt and shame from his actions upon the Mendap. He wept.

Eight harvest seasons had past when Rey wandered into the forest and discovered Drapo. He hoped something of value had remained. There was no sound, and he felt darkness in his spirit. Looking at his fathers remains still under the great crystal, he collapsed and began mourning for the first time. He grieved and wailed and moved in rage. When he could finally stop his weeping, he heard another person weeping nearby.

Turning slowly he could see Atpo, who could not meet his eyes. Atpo was becoming weak with age, and he softly begged Rey for forgiveness on behalf of himself and his people. "Forgiveness?" said Rey. "What you did was final and can never be undone."

Atpo could not look up and for a time the two stood still. Atpo broke the silence, saying, "My people have been shamed with guilt, for once we were the children of good parents." He continued, "Our life has been influenced by our past with the Mendap. I bear the guilt of our times of anger and it shall wither away with me. Our children are rich with wisdom from the wall that I have passed to them, and of the Mendap they have come to be."

Atpo led Rey to a place where his people worshiped. Overlooking the valleys and fields, in a quiet place in the foothills of the Celestereen, was a monument of stone taken from the forest by the Wall of Alling.

As Rey read the script on the stone, a new strength was born inside him. The words read, "The cold blooded killers deeds will never be undone. Their souls will never be freed. To our children, this we teach. We love, we are gentle. We are kind, caring and affectionate. Our children shall live and give. On this stone is inscribed our chore that another hurt be nevermore."

Returning to the remains of his father, Rey stopped in mid-thought. For two nights and a day, he was alone in vigil within the forest that was once his home. His father had taught him of the peaceful ways of fulfilling ones needs. The energy of Onway's spirit remained, and it passed to Rey's empty soul. With this, his destiny became eternally fixed by Trall.

At the light of the second day, Rey delivered the remains of Onwey to the river Osholan. Rey mounted Drapo once more and rode with sorrow, but he had peace inside. He rode to the Celestereen and to the sacred path of Trall. Onwey had led him to the start of the river long ago. Only those pure in heart and pure in soul were able to climb into the heavens with the insight of almighty souls.

Atpo found Drapo wandering about the hills. He led the steed to the valleys of harvest and allowed him move about and graze freely. Never again would one make seat on the steed.

Rey, hosted by Trall, was made an oversoul. The valleys and wood were now his responsibility. Balance would remain and all about the land would be kept good.

In the colder times, the valleys of the harvest would be lit with brilliant arches. Prismatic shows filled with color would span the skies, and the air would get warmer. The Raone called this the Reyal, or the gift of Rey. Sowing of seed would become dear as this meant the warmer season was near. The elders of the Rayone would make pilgrimage now, and into their past once again would know The Lesson of the Ash.

One Bundle Of Snow

Standing and looking for that one view so great
Peering through lens for some time in wait
A target in drift gray skies send this day
Journey to far below
One tiny bundle of snow

Focusing quick a descent in sight
To catch it before the changing twilight
Now in print this tiny parcel heaven sent
One bundle of snow to cause an event

To a black velvet shawl a thrown is found
At home alone, a vivid contrast is shown
A package of shapes
This one on black drape

Comes the first falling
And in spell all do see
One bundle of snow to be a lead
And so a following famous indeed

As next view is etched

Close friends now in frame

Chapel bell ring as passerby's sing

Night coming near and to gather all

Leaving for home and closing this roam

Tiny bundles of snow...the very first show

A Kitten Plays

All I want is for you to be
Happy once again
You had always been

It is not fair
You close to despair
So much I care
Won't let you there

Please try hard
A memory to see
Maybe for us
Once again pleasure would be

A short time you and me
And loneliness comes to be
I wish you be free
As a kitten plays
For you and for me

Unaware

No one knew the darkness within the guilt below her tantricity. To think that nobody wanted to was a determination born. To see her in feelings that marked despair. To know that she needed me, a friend, a friend for her own self, who she would allow to know her.

They stopped at a shop where pink snapdragons were wrapped in green tissue. They were kept cool on her lap as I started the car moving once again. The gate of the cemetery was calling to her confusion and forgetfulness.

Black and gray stones were about: some so pretty and some so elaborate and some so large and some so simple. One, just one, was calling to her fantasia. She had almost forgotten and was near broken down when her tears of long ago secrets and hurt never undone began to fall. I arranged the blooms in the small urns attached to her stone of salvation under which her mother rested.

She cried for the salvation from so long ago, and carved yellow roses told him to just let her be. I saw her anguish and let her see that she was there to grow. I begged her as I held her tight, "Do not be fooled by the pain you call death, but rather grow in all of its certainty and finality. You are not dying love, oh no, you have come back to the life of a cleansed spirit."

We relaxed in the evening in happier places, and on the face which earlier rained tears a smile slowly dawned. The smile was from the intrusion of memories fading back in her mind, and from her passing from unaware to be once again with the moment.

My compassion was a work lonely. Her wholeness once again became true. The night was long and detached in peace for us and from the world.

Tangle Inside

One spring day in town

Looking over and down

Soon to discover

Such love by one upholding another

Travel was short

Yet complex of sort

Around to a small road

Four riding

A sparse load

The family elder seeming alone

Tangled up pathways in mind did show

Sir driver you know

All safe to go

Later in day returning the same way

Few words could not hide

One fathers tangle inside

To push sadness aside

Was the work of pride

So quiet the air...and so too the pair

The End Of Patricia

If she arrives at beyond help
Will she always be there?
If she feels what is not
Will she lose all good thought?

Can her mind turn her page
Is there choice on another stage?
Can she shine?
Can foresight be hers and still in time

Hopeless sought in frustrations thought
If the page were turned to
Suffer she would not
If she were to know a light may show
If only in a moment she once
Again would glow

To wish her pages turn her days
To see some joy as she would play
Then truly all would be safe to say
Helplessness hopelessness
Could finally and always be wished away

In A Whisper

You beckon a treasure from afar
Perhaps it's in the nighttime sky
Perhaps it's somewhere on a star

Yes it was so bright a sight
Like one so long before at night
And so now most certainly I wonder of you
By the ways you hold me your love so new

Only for you and me to grow
Is a garden for only us to know
And beyond the joy of what we sow
From the garden of glory becomes our story

As a falling leaf falling on a pond of mirrors
Will create a pool for its very own
That moves out to make another found
And in so doing makes almost a sound
As do feelings treasured
As a rainbow from heaven
To encircle us to let us be
To let us be

Or maybe our garden is a glory of three

Is a road to journey for you and me

A bridge to cross and not to know

But being there with you to sow

Bouncing balls and autumn leafs

We watch them all and gather all

To hear them whisper

Let me hold you tight

Let me hold you tight each and every night

That our spirit anew be always bright

The treasured seeds the things we do

Heavenly glory

Our garden true

Trip My Fire In Echoes

Intoxicate me with kisses
Stagger me on your love and
Let me not care of
Anything but this.

Make my world disappear in a
Rhythm. Let us dance and
Sway me and rock me so.
Never to let go til the
Fire of our embrace
Stirs once again and I
Glow once again and again.

Once again let me feel your kiss,
Returning soft and gentle, to
Stagger me into bliss.

Please, when I can move no longer,
Just watch me at peace as the
Embers of our eloquence
Slowly cool from the joy of
You...

Among The Willows

Embrace me with your words
Words to hold my mind gently
As a mother holds her child
Her child at peace
At peace from love
From love so deserving

Sow skillfully your caring
With so gentle a touch
To grow me secure
In holding your spirit
And give this goodness
That it be mirrored

Let your words
Be so a romance
Of simple pleasure
To bring moments of ecstasy
As voices of kindness
Reaching each other
Willow within our souls

Petals Of The Daisy

Whistling is the wind
And through the trees my face becomes
A summer breeze.
Catch me please or shall I fall
As a lonely leaf to still water beneath.

Hear I am but know not time
And so my now is you in mind

A wintry blast and can I last
But wait tis June
And a warming moon.
I know you're mine within this rhyme.
I wait and pray
Once again to play.

See the daisy a smiling bloom.
Pull the petals you shall see me soon.
Summer, Fall, Winter and Spring
This rhyme is ours
You see…in time

Compose

So you come once again with only a song but a melody it makes and I wonder how long. Its notes you sing softly become so dear. Reach to my heartbeats, never so near. Compose a duet that our hearts mate in harmony. Compose every breath to fall into one quiet. Yes, etch on my spirit to sustain our love do. Write it quiet, write it tender, touch me softly let my soul always know. Compose us clearly again and again. Make us the air that only we do share,

Compose …compose

With Percale

Opal and onyx
Resting in curl
Whirling a sight
Pictures this night

Looking to one book
Thoughts many to see
Kindness and joy
Feelings come anew
Hopes and prayers
Seemingly true
Wondering why
Cause to cry

Trapped in a calm
Spin and weave
Slowly to warm
Opal and onyx
Whirling til morning

Where We Met

You met me in the willow
You met me in the rain
You met me where smiles are lost
Where frowns reflect the pain

We thought we knew the sadness
We shared of prisons past
Thought we'd finally met the one
Who'd understand at last

The blossoms of our friendship
The flowers and the moss
Became a kind of kinship
Of loved ones we had lost

While sitting in the meadow
We came to share a smile
For all the times we'd suffered
We'd been there all the while

By The Farm

If I were made of stone
Could you be touched by me?
And if I were to fall, I wonder,
Would you understand me?

If I were alone
Could you hear what I might say?
And if I were not near, I wonder,
Would you see me?

If I were a wall
Could you talk to me?
Would your good will become a habit?
Will you take the chance?
Will you be my friend? Neighbor

Angels In Mud

After listening to those strange sounds for days, we began to question them. They were especially noticeable early in the morning as they broke the serenity of the lake. A low scraping sound that was barely audible was followed by a loud knock that left a dead echo about the lake.

We had been at our new home about a week spending most of our time discovering our seemingly large new yard. A stone wall split the upper half and the lower half of the lawn. A stone stairway led up to the upper area where we found a shuffle board court. We discovered the game equipment in the garage. The garage was two floors and wide enough for two cars and storage. We played the game intensely every day.

I was nine and my sister, Lil, was seven. We made friends with Jim and Donna, who lived next door. Jim was also nine and Donna was also seven. They had moved to the lake that summer as well. The lake seemed awesome surrounded by big old pine trees, and people were water-skiing and boating and swimming and fishing.

Late in the morning, on our first Saturday, after we discovered the crooked lines on the shallow lake bottom were left by the clams moving at night, we decided to go and search for those sounds. It was after lunch when the four of us met on the unfinished road behind our homes. We were all from the city, so none of us could identify those odd sounds.

We started out on the road that was laded with rocky depressions and winding. Soon we came to a gate with a worn path to its side. We passed around and continued on. We came to a sharp turn in the road and could see the long well-kept beach at the end of the lake. There was nobody on the beach, which we thought it strange as we stared, but none of us spoke.

Our feet scraped the loose surface of the road as it started uphill. We followed it to the end, then turned left onto another rocky road that was even more unfinished and less traveled. After walking a short distance, the road opened up in front of us and a huge truck roared by. We stood behind some dwindling trees trying to hide. We were afraid that we would be in trouble for being there.

A short time passed, and it seemed quiet, so we crossed a well groomed gravel covered road. To our left we saw trucks dumping stones over an embankment. One truck was dumping boulders into a hole. We walked about two hundred yards past a big field to the right and SampSons Washed Sand and Gravel to the left.

We sat at the edge of a wooded area and watched wide eyed at what we thought of as an enormous erector set. All sizes of stone down to sand were being carried on wide belts. Two long parts that looked like screws pulled sand up and over to fall on the top of a pile that seemed one hundred feet high.

Suddenly everything stopped. Jim looked at his watch and said, "I think they are going home."

Lil and I looked at each other and I yelled "what a sand box!" We all laughed.

Soon it seemed that nobody was left down there. The small trucks and cars near the big garage were gone. It was quiet as we looked at a backwash swamp attached to the beginning of the lake from our perch.

Making our way down a long hill, and heading towards the swamp, we came to a pool. The pool was filled with foggy brown water. We walked around the embankment picking up stones and trying to skip them across the water. Most of them didn't make it and instead landed in the water with a splash.

We found a pipe at one end of the pool, and by following it, we discovered that it led to another pool. This second pool was a curiosity. There was no water in this one but just a thick, almost solid, brown substance.

We all wandered around the top of the embankment, which was about six feet high. We wondered just what that stuff was. Could we walk on it? Would we sink and get sucked into it and drown?

I became brave and made my way down to the edge of the pool. "It's cold," I yelled to them. Moving towards the center of the pool I was soon holding my pant legs at my knees. Five feet from the edge and I was already that deep. "Come on," I called, "It's clay." Lil, Donna, and Jim slid down to the edge to the clay pool. I moved back to the edge and took off my clothes. I waded back towards the middle and soon I was waist deep in the cold muck. In a few minutes we were all in the fine packed silt that had been washed from the sand and pumped into these pools to settle. Our legs created a low suction release sound as we tried to maneuver around the pool. We threw the mud around and tried to find out just how deep we could sink. We molded our hair into odd styles. Mine was sort of a rooster. Lil's was mud braids. We couldn't figure what Jim and Donna were doing with theirs but we laughed a lot. Donna laid back and moved her arms up and down and her legs open and shut. She made an angel in mud. She said, "It's the opposite of an angel in snow." We all joined in to make angels in mud.

We discovered that the deeper we sank the colder the clay and more thick it was. We would not sink. The wrestling to move was work that wore us down. I pulled Donna out twice because she was getting too tired. We decided our fun in the clay pool had to end.

I climbed the embankment and crossed a small access road to find the swamp and another pool. This one was different from the ones we had been at. The banks of this pool were below the water, and the water was clear. A rope hung over a path to the water and was tied to a tree. "Come on," I screamed, "you should see this." They came, dragging themselves across the road. Sliding down the short bank, we stooped into the water so it was at our shoulders. Relaxed, we shook the clay from our clothes and bodies. Soon the pool had become filled with a light brown fog.

We climbed back to the road and followed it to the beach. We swam one more time for a sort of final rinse. We then started walking the shoreline towards home. The lake was quiet, and I thought maybe tomorrow we would try and find the train line. It seemed every night a train roared through, and it seemed kind of near. We found where those strange sounds came from, but there were so many different things going on there that we just could not put them at a specific spot at SampSons. We slowly staggered seemingly intoxicated but truly exhausted from our day of exploring our new neighborhood and having so much fun.

On Evil

If you believe someone or something is telling you to do something bad or is doing something bad to you, understand these thoughts evolve out of feelings which are in truth distorted feelings you have about yourself. The power of these distorted feelings can be such that you may in truth hear them as a voice or voices. These negative feelings about yourself interrupt the successful dealing with your life. If this is you, then your self worth needs to be repaired for sure. Another name for distorted feelings, is feelings that are lying to you.

To deal with evil is to understand the word *no* in regards to yourself and others who may be harmed by your actions which is to say *no* to action and thinking which may harm your inside world and your outside world.

A young boy walked into school pulled out a gun and shot dead two of his classmates. Everybody thought he was responsible. He was but only in part. When he pulled the trigger he became responsible for making himself a cold blooded killer. The two classmates had been harassing him for years because their own self worth was dependant on being bullies. The parents of the two boys were in part responsible as they were ignorant to the harassment. The owner of the gun was partly responsible as the gun was available to the young man and the owner was ignorant to the harassing as well. The controversy centered on the gun. The truth was the gun was one of many choices.

Evil is a pressure on a thought which pushes aside the decision making process and moves you to take harmful action and without regard to yourself or others. Evil is not an emotion, however, it attaches to an emotion such as anger or hatred or love - his love for her was destroyed by his community so he in his turn tried to destroy the community. This of course does not work as in your community those who destroy are removed.

Employing self-control while learning to deal with your problems is to render evil harmless. Finding a good teacher to learn to deal with your problems is necessary.

On the heavens or on eight truths

Revelation One

We were called to the gym where a musical was to take place. It was a surprise of sorts. We all listened and the band was surely professional. The music was not of the sort that we would normally listen to after school with friends or at home. The music stopped and a musician asked us all to close our eyes and ask God to come into our lives and for a few moments there was silence. I asked this of God without hesitation nor doubt. I was fourteen and always remembered this asking of the unknown for the very first time. At times I wondered if I was the only one.

Revelation Two

Walking down the stairs to be outside I stood on the lawn and looked up at the stars. The stars seemed more bright than usual and larger just a bit. I was gazing upon them when from the corner of my eye I saw the figure of a man. I saw the figure move towards me and then into me. I felt a nervous shudder. I was fifteen and did not understand it. I spoke of it to nobody for thirty years and by some reason thought of the man as middle aged and dressed in a business suit.

Revelation Three

I didn't remember exactly when it started but that it was in the later days of the workshop. Those who were trying to help themselves, who were changing for the good I noticed. I brought forward in my mind a cross of gold and placed it upon their foreheads. They would not know and what the meaning in this was I was not sure.

Revelation Four

I was lying down resting when I saw to my right an apparition. She was robed in earth tones of dark tan and red and appeared immaculate. She made the sign of the cross to me and was gone. I did not know what to think or do. After some time I knew I had been blessed by who I began to think of as the blessing mother.

I still knew not what to do so I found the word blessed in a book. It read to be made holy or to be set aside for a holy mission. I still knew not what to do so I glanced around in my mind at my life as it were and decided that the only response I could have was to continue down the same road I had been on. That road was to continue trying to help my wife who had become ill and working and writing and visiting the workshop where others to include myself needed to continue to grow as well.

Revelation Five

As I listened to my brother talk about the rotary winged aircraft and point to the one he was hoping to pilot for the navy in a book he had drawn pictures of a priest entered the room. I faintly heard the priest ask that her sins be forgiven and an anger came over me. How could he know if she had sinned or if she had ever sinned. How was it good to say anything not good at such a time in such a place and in such company. The priest left as quickly as he arrived.

As I approached I stopped and looked at her for some time. My sister came to my side and we knelt down in front of her and said nothing. She left me and I stood and looked once again to see a cross of gold appear upon the side of her peaceful face and in my heart I knew what she always wanted when I leaned over and kissed her cheek. Her spirit ascended and I knew she did not know- that her body had died as it died in peace. As if torn away her face was in terror as she looked upon her body but nowhere else and was gone.

As I thought about her from time to time I came to believe that she needed affection. Maybe only from me and I thought it was good that she went up. I knew there were still so many uncertainties and that the truth about a few moments with the mother of my father were for me only. I thought upon a rainbow and wondered was this one on a clear day sent by a kiss.

Miracle One

It was a certainty that her life was to end within twenty four hours and as I stood outside her home and brought the universe into my self and thought the most holy words. I asked by the Blessing Mother to send a legion and for the power of Rapha-el so that her life not end. That she continue to heal others. That if there was dark evil on the land about that it be cleansed. That evolution not take her life when the angels came. Translucent of a sort as running tap water and passing down and through me and out and I knew I had been heard and that was good.

The sign on the door read do not disturb. It suddenly opened and her husband came out and into the street where I stood. There was a brief greeting that ended with the words Joy and Peace.

It was three weeks past when I returned to that neighborhood. After a visit with my brother I started walking home when I turned to see her coming from behind driving her van and our smiles met. I wondered as she passed by if she was saved for a particular mission or was it that she would continue healing as the nurse she truly was.

Miracle Two

As we sat at the table my sister started to pray in thanks for the food which was on it. I had trouble understanding this as it was by the power of my sister and her family that the food was there. I knew they were in need but that their needs were not in food. I brought the universe into my self once again and thought the most holy words. I asked of the Blessing Mother to send help to my sister's family and cleanse their home of any dark evil and favor the family of my sister. The heavens came close and the angels came once again and appeared translucent as running water and flying down and out through me. One particularly noticeable went to the side of me which was where the older of my nieces was sitting.

I thought all would be good now. So keeping this to myself as we had feast I made remark to my sister that she would know her own power and not give it up to God. That God does not want it but rather she need master her own. And that was my advice on that day.

Later during the visit the mother of my sisters husband arrived and so he spoke to her of seeing the Blessing Mother. I said nothing as what he saw was for him only. A road for him may have been put down on that day.

Revelation Six

As I sat with a loved one and as we discussed the end of the behavioral services wing of the hospital I fell into prayer. I brought the universe into my self once again and asked the Holy Mother to bring the power of Rapha-el and relieve the hospital of it's selfish past when upon my mind in a sudden came a vision. I saw Rapha-el standing fifty feet tall in the courtyard of the hospital. He was robed and appeared immaculate. From his feet came up and out in all directions from the earth countless souls which were a sort of earth tone, a lighter shade of tan. I did not know what this meant. The souls had no distinguishing marks and all edges of their human shape were rounded. The vision lasted but a few seconds and then I was in fatigue.

My love was an artist and after some time I drew a sketch of what I had seen and showed her asking if she had ever seen such a picture. She said no. I did not know what to think about it so we decided to do nothing but continue on the road of our lives for the time being.

No divine intervention told me to write these pages. No divine intervention told me do not write them. To you my experiences are opinion or perception or dream. To me it is part of my truth.

Seeing what is, is not seeing only what you want to see.

The unknown is as much a part of humankind as humankind is a part of the unknown this is the Thirteenth Iron Law.

Which is as individual as it is universal.

If your perception of your world or your outside world is distorted so too will be the change that is the outcome of the choices you then take.

As Joy Travels

Peace was quiet as Joy left to search for a loss. Joy invited Creativity to travel along as they were close to each other. Creativity said, "I will travel with you Joy," and the traveling began.

Creativity occupied most of the time thinking. Creativity sometimes would think in questions. Questions such as: What may be created next? Will more joy be created? Will next come to an end at some time?

After traveling for a long while with Joy, Creativity could see Choice. Creativity asked Joy if Choice could travel along as well. Joy could feel how important Choice was. Choice joined the traveling group. Joy, Creativity and Choice traveled together.

Choice spoke to Creativity and Joy, "I will never leave, and I am vulnerable as both good and bad, to any degree, will flow from me."

Creativity turned to Choice and reported, "I am always trying to limit myself. Humankind has some of me as Joy desires someone to create what may bring one Joy.

Joy, Creativity and choice continued traveling. Joy felt the loss. People were hurting each other, and hurting themselves as well. Joy suddenly left Creativity and Choice.

Joy found a special place where a community was gathered. There Joy commanded, "do not" in regards to bad, evil and destructive things people were doing to themselves and others. It was a desperate time for Joy.

Joy left and found Choice and Creativity. They traveled together once again. Soon Joy left Creativity and Choice a second time. Joy felt more loss. Hurt was being created by many people.

Joy found a woman and gave her a son. Joy was with him as he grew and never left. The son was a reflection of Joy, and he spoke to the community about Joy and Peace: that Joy comes from Peace. He said to many people, "be that I am, I am what I love to do. I love to feel Joy and be with Peace. There is hurt, evil and destruction, of which I am not." He continued, "and comes from you the decision making process. This you give to yourselves. The degrees of good and bad flow from your action or your decision not to act."

In the audience had been a man that scribed the words spoken by the son of Joy, and the words were preserved. Some of the words became a way for one to talk to Joy about Creativity and Choice and what may flow from his or her decisions. The words were a way to talk to Joy for the sake of Joy. The words were a way to make contact with Joy.

The son of Joy was destroyed by his community because he was a reflection of Joy. He was destroyed in part because his community believed he had no authority to teach about Joy. His community was given a choice, and it chose to destroy him so that bad and evil should live. Joy could not understand why one would want to destroy Joy and hurt Peace as well. Joy left to find Choice and Creativity.

Joy found Creativity holding Choice. The first tears of sadness on the traveling had fallen. Choice was close to despair and no longer desired to exist. Joy held Creativity and Choice, and Choice became strong once again. Choice asked Joy, "how can I ever find Resolve?" Joy then spoke, "He was destroyed because living for something greater than themselves was unimportant. Joy, that I am, and Peace was not learned by all. Before his life ended, he asked me to forgive those who destroyed him, and that I am. I can not forgive those who destroy life. His destruction belongs to those who took the action upon their own decision. Stay with us Choice; remember the process of decision is not yours, and an amount of me remains. You will always be growing, be patient."

Joy then spoke to Creativity, "let there be pain in grief that one be moved to find truth, and let truth lead one back to the ground of love from where one shall heal and one shall grow."

The traveling continued once more. Creativity and Choice continued to grow. The amount of good and bad did as well.

Creativity became more fragile, as Choice was growing so fast. Creativity surely understood that Choice would never stop growing. Creativity also understood that the more Choice would grow, the more complex Choice would become.

Joy would look back from time to time, and there was indeed Joy to a degree. Soon Joy understood that no matter how much bad, evil and destruction may flow from a decision acted upon, or a decision not to act, one thing would always remain. Joy announced, "The good is immortal."

Creativity suddenly spoke, "There is Hope." Joy, Creativity and Choice beckoned Hope to join in the traveling. Hope understood Choice and said, "here is indeed where I belong."

Joy could feel that Hope secured Choice, as Hope spoke to Choice saying, "If in the process of decision only good is sought as the outcome, I will return good to the same degree. What is bad, evil or destructive done by any individual is selfish, and I may become overwhelmed. I may need to leave and be with Peace."

Joy spoke to Hope, "It is good to have you traveling with us. The decision making process is for humankind only. What flows from action or no action on a decision creates the degrees of both good and bad.

Choice then spoke, "It is a clouded view in reflection now."

Joy suddenly ordered, "Do not look back. Reflection is for humankind to learn from and for Hope to visit. You will always be related to decision Choice, and Hope will always be near."

Hope embraced Choice and softly spoke, "You are safer now. Remember where I come from, because in that there is no choice. I will always be with you as we travel."

Joy, feeling a kinship with Choice and Hope, spoke to them, "Wherever you may be, Choice, what ever may flow from a decision by any one individual, is a reflection of me in humankind. It is you, Hope, that shall bring me back to Peace. I miss her so very much."

Respectfully So

This Fine Young Tree

A Fare Unfair

Negamation

At The Lot On The Job

The Storm The Stars And Play In the Yard

Master Of Reception

The Accommodation

To Whom It May Concern

The Continuous Growing Process

Fresh Air

Dancing

Dilemma

Languor

Let Her Go

Belief In Action

Accordingly

Hills And Valleys

Belief

About My Lamp

Chained

Light A Candle

From The Altar At Francis Gate

When I want To Write

Mirror Of Toil

Hello Cousin

My Dear Sister

Dear Mom And dad

Mary Lou

Open The day

By The Ocean

In Island

Shattered Glass

A Different Path

We Just Try To Help

Wendy

Hello There

By The Phone

Iced Coffee, Peanut Butter And Jelly

Best Friend

Dancing

She Wants The Sky

The Lesson Of The Ash

One Bundle Of Snow

A Kitten Plays

Unaware

Tangle Inside

The End Of Patricia

In A Whisper

Trip My Fire In Echo's

Among The Willows

Petals Of The Daisy

Compose

With Percale

Where We Met

By The Farm

Angels In Mud

On Evil

On The Heavens Or Eight Truths

Revelation One

Revelation Two

Revelation Three

Revelation Four

Revelation Five

Miracle One

Miracle Two

Revelation Six

The Thirteenth Iron Law

As Joy Travels

I am grateful for the consistent interest and loving perception of Patricia Burke during the Process of the final efforts about this book Where We Met appears courtesy of Patricia Burke.

About the Author

Mark Loiselle was born in Lowell Massachusetts to loving parents who nurtured him with care by giving him much freedom to learn from friends and chance. As a child he loved to explore where his legs would take him. His parents exposed him to the arts and sports as well. He is among four sisters and three brothers. Mark currently lives in Lowell. In high school he was devastated by a social phobia which continued for around twenty years. Mark graduated from high school in 1973. From then to 1975 Mark was hospitalized four times before treatment for bi-polar disorder became effective. He has been in treatment as an outpatient since then. The phobia and many other social problems were fixed along the way with the help of many good people.

Mark has had many jobs and among them were tree work, a desk job at a computer company and an assistant grower all of which he liked. Mark has been using disability insurance and driving a small truck part time. About the job he says, "I can live with it and that is what matters because being a part of the labor force is important." Mark usually writes at night when he gets ideas and finishes his work in the morning, as he says, "with a clear mind."

Printed in the United States
21274LVS00004B/76-78

9 781418 438524